The WORKS OF MERCY

By Rev. LAWRENCE G. LOVASIK, S.V.D.

CATHOLIC BOOK PUBLISHING CORP., New Jersey

Jesus Teaches about the Works of Mercy

Jesus speaks:

"WHEN the Son of Man comes in His glory, with all the angels of heaven, He will sit upon His royal throne, and all the nations will be assembled before Him.

CPSIA   July 2010   10 9 8 7 6 5 4 3 2   A/P

"The king will say to those on His right: 'Come. You have My Father's blessing! Inherit the Kingdom prepared for you from the creation of the world. For I was hungry and you gave Me food, I was thirsty and you gave Me drink. I was a stranger and you welcomed Me; naked and you clothed Me. I was ill and you comforted Me, in prison and you came to visit Me.'

"Then the just will ask Him: 'Lord, when did we see You hungry and feed You or see You thirsty and give You drink? When did we welcome You away from home or clothe You in Your nakedness? When did we visit You when You were ill or in prison?'

"The King will answer them: 'I assure you, as often as you did it for one of My least brothers, you did it for Me.'

"The just will go off to eternal life."

(Matthew 25:31-40)

Michael collects money to help
feed the starving people of the world.

1st CORPORAL WORK OF MERCY

To Feed the Hungry

Jesus speaks:

"I was hungry and you gave Me food."

(Matthew 25:35)

THERE are many millions of people to-day who are very hungry because they are poor. Some children can get less than one meal a day. Our country sends them food and clothing. Many die of starvation.

Naturally, you feel sorry for them and try to help them by praying for them. But you can also collect money for them which can be sent to some missionaries or to the Bishop of the diocese.

This is one way by which you can show God that you love your neighbor and that you are thankful of the good food your parents give you every day. Food is a gift of God and you must thank Him for it.

5

Billy and Marie share their lunch at school
with Timmy whose family is poor.

To Give Drink to the Thirsty

Jesus speaks:

"I was thirsty and you gave Me drink."

(Matthew 25:35)

JESUS once said: "I promise that whoever gives a cup of cold water to the least of My followers because that person is My follower will certainly receive a reward." (Matthew 10:42).

By these words Jesus taught us to be kind to people when they are in need. Giving a thirsty person a drink of water is a kind deed and Jesus will reward it.

You can do many favors for people who need your help. There are many children in the world who are hungry and thirsty. Pray for them.

Be kind to your playmates, too. Be willing to share your food and drink with them. This is a work of mercy if you do these things for the love of Jesus as He asked You to do.

Helen and John are bringing their used clothes to the Sisters at the Orphanage to help poor children.

To Clothe the Naked

Jesus speaks:

"I was naked and you clothed Me."

(Matthew 25:35)

THERE are many poor people who need clothing. Your mother and father buy such beautiful clothes for you to wear. Do you ever think of the many children who have to wear old and torn clothes, even rags?

Why don't you ask your mother to collect all your clothes which you hardly ever wear or which are too small for you so that you can give them to some poor child who needs them?

You can always bring used clothes to the St. Vincent de Paul Society collection box in your parish. Your parish priest or your teacher will tell you what to do with them. Each year before Thanksgiving Day, parishes have clothes collection drives for the poor. Do your part to help them.

Jerry visits his friend Andy who was sent to a Reform School. He brings him a rosary and prayerbook and asks him to pray to God and the Blessed Virgin for help.

4th CORPORAL WORK OF MERCY

To Visit Those Who Are in Prison

Jesus speaks:

"I was in prison and you came to visit Me."
(Matthew 25:36)

THERE are many children who are in Reform Schools. Why don't you and some of your friends visit them sometime? This will show them that you really care about them.

But there are many men and women in prisons all over our country. You cannot visit them, but you can pray for them that they may try to live a good life by turning to God in prayer. God alone can help them to be good.

Thank God for having given you good parents and teachers to lead you on the right path. God has commanded you to be obedient to them in His Fourth Commandment: "Honor your father and mother."

Donna welcomes a poor family to her home for dinner.

12

5th CORPORAL WORK OF MERCY

To Shelter the Homeless

Jesus speaks:

"I was a stranger and you welcomed Me."

(Matthew 25:36)

THERE are many poor people in the world who do not have a beautiful home like you have. How thankful you should be to God for all that your mother and father have done to make you happy! How good it is to have a nice warm home in winter!

Never be ashamed to bring poor children to your home. Since you have been so blessed by God, you should at least pray for those who do not have a home like yours.

Even though you cannot share your home with others, you can be kind to people everyday by helping them in small ways and trying to make them happy. If you do this for others, you do it for Jesus. He will reward you for being generous.

Joseph and his sister Elizabeth bring some food
to two old people in the neighborhood.

6th CORPORAL WORK OF MERCY

To Visit the Sick

Jesus speaks:

"I was ill and you comforted Me."

(Matthew 25:36)

THERE are many sick people in your neighborhood whom you can visit. You can make them very happy just by coming to talk to them for a while. They are often very lonely.

Old people also like company because they are often left alone. You can ask your mother to give you some food for them. She will be happy to see that you care for others.

In this way you can be like Jesus Who spent so much time healing the sick. Visit the sick and old people for the love of Jesus.

Someday you will be sick and grow old, and you will be pleased when someone comes to visit you and cheer you up. Be a friend of those who are sick and lonely, and you will be a friend of Jesus,

Raymond and his sister Rose like to take care
of the grave of their grandmother.

To Bury the Dead

Jesus speaks:

"I am the Resurrection and the Life. Whoever believes in Me, though he should die, will come to life." (Jn 11:25-26)

AFTER Martha and Mary, the sisters of Lazarus, had buried their brother, Jesus consoled them by telling them that He Himself is the Resurrection and the Life. Even though their brother died, Jesus raised him to life again.

Jesus will also console us when our loved ones die. We all shall live forever because of our faith in Jesus. But we must pray for our dead, attend their funeral when we can, and visit their grave to show that we really love them even though they are no more with us.

The Church remembers the dead by offering Holy Mass for them. She remembers the Poor Souls in Purgatory especially in the month of November and on All Souls Day.

Bob tells Fred that it is wrong to fight.

The 7 Spiritual Works of Mercy

1st SPIRITUAL WORK OF MERCY

To Admonish the Sinner

Jesus speaks:

"There will be joy among the angels of God over one repentant sinner." (Luke 15:10)

JESUS Christ came into the world as God made man, to be its Savior and Redeemer. God so loved sinners that He gave His Son to make peace between God and all people by His death on the Cross. Jesus often spoke to sinners to help them give up their evil ways.

If Jesus loved sinners so much, you should try to help them by your prayers and sacrifices. You can also speak kindly to other children when you see they are doing wrong.

Fred hit Bob with a bat. Bob was not angry, but he told Fred that it was wrong to fight. Susan, Bob's sister, wiped her brother's bleeding head and also told Fred not to fight anymore.

Karen tells Pat that it is a serious sin to miss
Mass on Sunday through his own fault.

To Instruct the Ignorant

Jesus speaks:

"Your light must shine before men so that they may see goodness in your acts and give praise to your heavenly Father."

(Matthew 5:16)

JESUS teaches us that the best way to instruct the ignorant is to give them a good example. A good deed is like light which shines in the minds of people and makes them want to do good and stay away from evil.

Karen stopped her friend Pat when she saw him riding his bicycle instead of going to Mass on Sunday. Karen told him that it was a great sin against God not to go to church on Sunday or Saturday evening.

Pat did not think it was too bad to miss Mass. He remembered Karen's words and never missed Mass again. The light of Karen's good example helped Pat to do what was right.

Billy asks Betty whether it is wrong to mow the lawn on Sunday. She tells him it is all right if he does it to get some exercise.

To Counsel the Doubtful

Jesus speaks:

"If you wish to enter into life, keep the Commandments." (Matthew 19:17)

A MAN once came up to Jesus and said: "Teacher, what good must I do to possess everlasting life." Jesus told him to obey the Commandments of God: to love God and his neighbor. The man was not sure what he had to do till Jesus showed him the right way to reach heaven.

It was Sunday. Billy's parents were out of town visiting friends. He asked his sister, Betty, whether it would be wrong for him to mow the lawn to get some exercise instead of playing ball with his friends.

Betty told him that it would be all right. Billy was then able to get his exercise with a clear conscience.

Kathy tries to cheer her sister up when she dropped her ice cream cone.

24

4th SPIRITUAL WORK OF MERCY

To Comfort the Sorrowful

Jesus speaks:

"Come to Me, all you who are weary and find life burdensome, and I will refresh you." (Matthew 11:28)

JESUS tells us that He will comfort us when we are sorrowful if only we come to Him asking for His help in prayer. Many things can happen in your life that can make you sad. Go to Jesus, your best Friend, and He will give you peace and joy. He will help you to be patient when you have something to suffer.

Be like Jesus. Try to cheer your friends up when they are sad.

Kathy tried to comfort her sister when she dropped her ice cream cone. Kathy even offered Mary her own cone. Mary stopped crying and was glad to share the cone with Kathy.

Ann tried to love Frank even though he smashed her baby buggy.

To Bear Wrongs Patiently

Jesus speaks:

"My command to you is: 'love your enemies, pray for your persecutors.'"

(Matthew 5:44)

JESUS teaches us to be patient when others hurt us, and even to pray for them. We cannot always like our enemies, but we must love them for the love of God.

One day Frank was so angry that he smashed Ann's baby buggy. Ann was hurt, but she did not get angry at Frank. She did not fight back to get even with him. She told him that they would still be friends and that her Daddy would fix the broken buggy.

Ann did not like Frank for what he did, but she tried to love him because she knew that this is what Jesus wanted her to do. She bore this wrong patiently. Try to do the same when someone hurts you.

Jesus said: "Treat others the way you would have them treat you."

Steve asks Mike and Joe to stop fighting and to forgive each other.

To Forgive Injuries

Jesus speaks:

"If you forgive the faults of others, your Heavenly Father will forgive you yours. If you do not forgive others, neither will your Father forgive you." (Matthew 6:14)

JESUS taught us to pray: "Forgive us our trespasses as we forgive those who trespass against us." You say this prayer every day when you say the "Our Father."

How can you expect the Heavenly Father to forgive your sins if you do not want to forgive others when they hurt you?

Mike and Joe got into a fight and were calling each other bad names because they were very angry at each other. Steve separated them and told them to shake hands and make up. They did. They became friends because they were willing to forgive each other.

The best way to help people, living and dead,
is to offer Holy Mass for them. Holy Mass is
the Greatest Prayer because it is the Sacrifice
of Jesus.

7th SPIRITUAL WORK OF MERCY

To Pray for the Living and the Dead

Jesus speaks:

"Ask, and you will receive. Seek, and you will find. Knock, and it will be opened to you. For the one who asks, receives. The one who seeks, finds. The one who knocks, enters. (Matthew 7:7)

GOD is Our Heavenly Father. He loves us as His children and wants to give us everything we need for our soul and body. But He wants us to ask for it.

Pray for your mother and father, brothers and sisters, relatives and friends, and for all who are in need of God's help, that they may reach heaven someday.

Pray also for those who have died, especially for your family, relatives, and friends. If they are in Purgatory, your prayers will help them to see God in heaven. The best way to help them is by offering Holy Mass for them.

A PRAYER OF THANKS FOR ANIMALS

ETERNAL Father, in Your wisdom and love You created the whole world. You told Adam to be the master of all the animals You made. Help me to be kind not only to people, but also to animals. Thank You for all the living things You made, especially for our pets.